I'M DREA
RED & WHITE
CHRISTMAS

BY ROGER MCCARTNEY

Independent Author

ISBN: 9781708606299

I'M DREAMING OF A RED & WHITE CHRISTMAS
BY ROGER McCARTNEY
On our first date you wore a home shirt.
On our second date you wore an away shirt.
On our third date I thought " Oh wow, the home shirt again"
And on our fourth date I thought: He has two shirts.

I'M DREAMING
OF A
RED & WHITE
CHRISTMAS
BY
ROGER
MCCARTNEY
So, honestly, do you think we've got a chance of finishing top four?
Listen, there's more chance of me being abducted by aliens.
A STOCKING FILLER
GIFT-BOOK
FOR RED & WHITE
FOOTBALL FANS

I'M DREAMING OF A RED & WHITE CHRISTMAS
BY ROGER MCCARTNEY
Never mind Andy Carroll, your injury won't last forever.
I know.
So why the long face?
A STOCKING FILLER GIFT-BOOK FOR RED & WHITE FOOTBALL FANS

I'M DREAMING OF A RED & WHITE CHRISTMAS
BY ROGER MCCARTNEY
Listen, if we get knocked out of the FA Cup, are you going to be ok?
Oh sure. It's only the FA cup.
He'll cry himself to sleep every night!

I'M DREAMING OF A RED & WHITE CHRISTMAS
BY ROGER MCCARTNEY
I'm so upset. I don't think I can go on!
Why, what's up?
I've just heard we might be buying Saido Berahino.

I'M DREAMING OF A RED & WHITE CHRISTMAS
BY ROGER MCCARTNEY
The number of chavs who support our club is starting to piss me off!
Me too bruv!
They're everywhere.

I'M DREAMING OF A RED & WHITE CHRISTMAS
BY ROGER MCCARTNEY
My dog attacks people if Spurs lose.
What does he do if they win?
I don't know. We've only had him 3 months!

I'M DREAMING OF A RED & WHITE CHRISTMAS
BY ROGER MCCARTNEY
You were on the M1 last night, coming home from the match weren't you?
Apparently, there was a driver going the wrong way.
One? I saw hundreds!

CHRISTMAS
Slow down! We want to get to the match in one piece!
Who's going to worry about us in this vintage car?
BY ROGER MCCARTNEY
POLICE SIREN!!!
Bit of a Lewis Hamilton are we Sir?
POLICE

I'M DREAMING OF A RED & WHITE CHRISTMAS
BY ROGER MCCARTNEY
Have you heard a big cat has been seen in the stand?
Yeah, do they expect us to believe that?
GONE!!
A STOCKING FILLER GIFT-BOOK FOR RED & WHITE FOOTBALL FANS

I'M DREAMING OF A RED & WHITE CHRISTMAS
BY ROGER MCCARTNEY
My wife is fed up with me, she wanted to have a chat last night.
Oh no, what about?
She reckons I'm childish. I just think about football all the time.
How did the talk go?
It didn't. I never let her in my fort.

I'M DREAMING OF A RED & WHITE CHRISTMAS
BY ROGER MCCARTNEY
If we don't finish top four this season, I'm going to eat my hat!
Where's your hat?
What hat?
A STOCKING FILLER GIFT-BOOK FOR RED & WHITE FOOTBALL FANS

I'M DREAMING OF A RED & WHITE CHRISTMAS
BY ROGER MCCARTNEY
I love you and don't ever want to be without you.
Do you mean that or are you just happy that your team won?
I was talking to the team!
FOR RED & WHITE FOOTBALL FANS

I'M DREAMING OF A RED & WHITE CHRISTMAS
BY ROGER MCCARTNEY
If you could have any player come to our club, who would it be?
I'd like to get Messi.
We'll have a drink later. Who would you have?
A STOCKING FILLER GIFT-BOOK FOR RED & WHITE FOOTBALL FANS

I'M DREAMING OF A RED & WHITE CHRISTMAS
BY ROGER MCCARTNEY
Lovely day for a drive to the match.
BANG!
FOR RED & WHITE FOOTBALL FANS

I'M DREAMING OF A RED & WHITE CHRISTMAS
BY ROGER MCCARTNEY
Do you wanna come over tonight?
Nah, I'm gonna stay in and watch the football.
The kids are at their dad's and i'm feeling dirty.
Ok, I'll bring the lads round to watch the football, while you have a bath then!

I'M DREAMING
OF A
RED & WHITE
CHRISTMAS
BY
ROGER
MCCARTNEY
Well, if we lose Saturday, we'll be drinking in the last-chance saloon.
I told Ron and Rosy we would met them in the King's Head!
A STOCKING FILLER GIFT-BOOK FOR RED & WHITE FOOTBALL FANS

I'M DREAMING
OF A
RED & WHITE
CHRISTMAS
BY
ROGER
MCCARTNEY
Crouchy, even you must agree you're too old to play.
Yes.
So, why the long face?
GIFT-BOOK
FOR RED & WHITE
FOOTBALL FANS

I'M DREAMING OF A RED & WHITE CHRISTMAS
BY ROGER MCCARTNEY
For Christmas day, I've got some news: I'm going to watch the under 15's.
For Christmas day, I've got a magic trick: POOF! You're single!
A STOCKING FILLER GIFT-BOOK FOR RED & WHITE FOOTBALL FANS

I'M DREAMING OF A RED & WHITE CHRISTMAS
BY ROGER MCCARTNEY
Man City away next week.
Are we going with two up front?
I'd start with two in goal, to be honest.
A STOCKING FILLER GIFT-BOOK FOR RED & WHITE FOOTBALL FANS

I'M DREAMING OF A RED & WHITE CHRISTMAS
BY ROGER MCCARTNEY
Just think of all the things that didn't exist 12 years ago.
Facebook, Twitter, YouTube, Instagram, Whatsapp, Uber, Snapchat..
...and Manchester City fans!

I'M DREAMING OF A RED & WHITE CHRISTMAS

I'M DREAMING OF A RED & WHITE CHRISTMAS
BY ROGER MCCARTNEY
I think we should try some role-reversal in bed.
What, you want me to have the headache and you wear the number 10 shirt?

I'M DREAMING OF A RED & WHITE CHRISTMAS
BY ROGER MCCARTNEY
Are you coming to watch the ladies tonight? We've got the Milwall Lionesses.
Leave it out! We never go and watch them.
Yeah but the Lionesses have got a new player.
What time you picking me up?

I'M DREAMING OF A RED & WHITE CHRISTMAS
BY ROGER MCCARTNEY
I hope we don't get Millwall again this season.
Christ no!
You know why they chant "oo are ya" at us? They're looking for their dads!
A STOCKING FILLER GIFT-BOOK FOR RED & WHITE FOOTBALL FANS

I'M DREAMING OF A RED & WHITE CHRISTMAS
BY ROGER MCCARTNEY
What's the matter sweet?
Well, if I,m honest, I'm annoyed with you.
Why?
You think more of your football club than you do me.
Don't be silly...
..I think more of Hartlepool United than I do you love!

I'M DREAMING
OF A
RED & WHITE
CHRISTMAS
BY
ROGER
McCARTNEY
Name three teams with swear words in their name.
Um, Arsenal....
..Scunthorpe...
...and Manchester fucking City!
A STOCKING FILLER
GIFT-BOOK
FOR RED & WHITE
FOOTBALL FANS

I'M DREAMING
OF A
RED & WHITE
CHRISTMAS

I'M DREAMING
OF A
RED & WHITE
CHRISTMAS
BY
ROGER
MCCARTNEY
I've ordered a brand new 72 inch telly for you to watch your soaps on.
That's so thoughtful. When's it coming?
In time for the Boxing Day match.
FOOTBALL FANS

I'M DREAMING OF A RED & WHITE CHRISTMAS
BY ROGER MCCARTNEY
My wife said what do I like best: her or football.
I said open your legs and I'll show you. So, she opened her legs ....
...and I nutmegged her. Get in! One-nil!
I'M DREAMING OF A RED & WHITE CHRISTMAS

I'M DREAMING OF A RED & WHITE CHRISTMAS
BY ROGER MCCARTNEY
Where do you want to go New Year's Eve?
Somewhere expensive.
Old Trafford?
GIFT-BOOK FOR RED & WHITE FOOTBALL FANS

I'M DREAMING OF A RED & WHITE CHRISTMAS
BY ROGER MCCARTNEY
That was lovely when you caressed me all over when we were in bed watching Match of The Day last night.
But why did you stop?
I found the remote!
FOOTBALL FANS

I'M DREAMING OF A RED & WHITE CHRISTMAS
BY ROGER MCCARTNEY
Now it's international weekend , I had a chat with the girlfriend last night.
Oh yeah? How did it go?
Yeah good. She seems like a nice person.
FOR RED & WHITE FOOTBALL FANS

I'M DREAMING OF A RED & WHITE CHRISTMAS

I'M DREAMING OF A RED & WHITE CHRISTMAS
BY ROGER MCCARTNEY
Is it true that men think about football every six seconds?
No of course not, that's the biggest load of rubb...
What was I saying?

I'M DREAMING OF A RED & WHITE CHRISTMAS
BY ROGER MCCARTNEY
What's the matter sis?
Well, you know how experimental I am?
I told him I wouldn't mind being taken up the shithole.
He took me to Goodison Park.

I'M DREAMING
OF A
RED & WHITE
CHRISTMAS
BY
ROGER
MCCARTNEY
The Spurs souvenir shop got broken into the other night.
I know, some cash and a load of replica shirts got taken.
The next night, they broke back in and put back the shirts!
A STOCKING FILLER
GIFT-BOOK
FOR RED & WHITE
FOOTBALL FANS

I'M DREAMING OF A RED & WHITE CHRISTMAS
BY ROGER MCCARTNEY
I got done for speeding again!
Another three points!
Nathan Jones rang me up the next day and asked me for some tips.
A STOCKING FILLER GIFT-BOOK FOR RED & WHITE FOOTBALL FANS

I'M DREAMING OF A RED & WHITE CHRISTMAS
BY ROGER MCCARTNEY
We're going to miss the match if the train don't get here soon.
What time is the next...
378 001

I'M DREAMING OF A RED & WHITE CHRISTMAS
BY ROGER MCCARTNEY
Sue was complaining that I never listen to her again. Said I don't listen to her but think about football constantly.
BY ROGER MCCARTNEY
Or something like that.

I'M DREAMING
OF A
RED & WHITE
CHRISTMAS
BY
ROGER
MCCARTNEY
I've just heard who we've got in the third round.
Hartlepool United.
BY
ROGER
MCCARTNEY
Thank you God.
FOOTBALL FANS

I'M DREAMING OF A RED & WHITE CHRISTMAS

I'M DREAMING
OF A
RED & WHITE
CHRISTMAS
BY
ROGER
MCCARTNEY
Besides football, what else do think about all day?
I hope your're not one of them brain dead blokes that only think about Women and football.
Of course not!
She's looking fit today. Who we got Saturday?
FOR RED & WHITE
FOOTBALL FANS

I'M DREAMING OF A RED & WHITE CHRISTMAS
BY ROGER MCCARTNEY
What do you want for Christmas then sonny?
A unicorn.
Be realistic.
Well, winning the league this season would be nice.
What colour unicorn?
A STOCKING FILLER GIFT-BOOK FOR RED & WHITE FOOTBALL FANS

I'M DREAMING OF A RED & WHITE CHRISTMAS
BY ROGER MCCARTNEY
Some eastern european blokes pushed me over on the way into the ground.
Were they Russian?
They were in a hurry, as it goes.
A STOCKING FILLER GIFT-BOOK FOR RED & WHITE FOOTBALL FANS

Made in the USA
Middletown, DE
18 December 2019

81342086R00027